This journal
belongs to

_____

iShine
JOURNAL

BroadStreet Publishing™
Racine, WI 53403
Broadstreetpublishing.com

iShine JOURNAL

© 2014 by BroadStreet Publishing

ISBN 978-1-4245-4931-3

All rights reserved. No part of this book may be reproduced in any form, except for brief quotations in printed reviews, without permission in writing from the publisher.

Quotations by Brad Mathias and Bema Media LLC, PO Box 670, Sherman TX 75091. Used by permission.

Scripture quotations from The Holy Bible, New International Version® (NIV®). Copyright © 1973, 1978, 1984, 2011 by Biblica, Inc.® All rights reserved worldwide. The Holy Bible, New King James Version® (NKJV). Copyright © 1982 by Thomas Nelson, Inc. The Holy Bible, English Standard Version® (ESV®), copyright © 2001 by Crossway Bibles, a publishing ministry of Good News Publishers. The New American Standard Bible® (NASB). Copyright © 1960, 1962, 1963, 1968, 1971, 1972, 1973, 1975, 1977, 1995 by The Lockman Foundation. The Holy Bible, New Living Translation (NLT). Copyright © 1996, 2004, 2007 by Tyndale House Foundation. Used by permission of Tyndale House Publishers, Inc., Carol Stream, Illinois 60188. The Message (MSG). Copyright © 1993, 1994, 1995, 1996, 2000, 2001, 2002. Used by permission of NavPress Publishing Group. All rights reserved.

Compiled by Michelle Winger
Design by Chris Garborg | www.garborgdesign.com

Printed in China.

iShine is a part of a faith-based ministry and media company focused on equipping pre-teens (tweens) and their families to find their value, identity, and purpose (VIP) in Christ. iShine is actively reaching today's tweens in a variety of ways including the following:

- Live events and concerts with our annual national tour, iShine LIVE!
- Syndicated National TV with our sitcom series iShine KNECT TV
- Tween Record Label with our contemporary Christian music group in Nashville, TN
- iShine Radio – a web-based professionally produced 24/7 FREE tween radio station available at iShinelive.com
- An extensive, interactive social media presence with Amazon.com, iDisciple, YouTube, Twitter, and Facebook (designed and updated weekly for tweens and their families)
- iShine HQ – a daily-devotional video series designed for tweens, their parents, and pastors (available for free at iShinelive.com)

To discover more about iShine, take a minute to check out our tween website, iShinelive.com, or stop by our parent-and-pastor site, ishineministries.com, and let us know what you think.

Blessings to you from the iShine staff and crew!

Spend some time with God and He'll reassure you that He has a plan for you.

For you created my inmost being;
you knit me together in my mother's womb.
I praise you because I am fearfully and wonderfully made;
your works are wonderful,
I know that full well.

PSALM 139:13-14 NIV

Your identity is in Christ. Period. At the very center of this message of being valued, loved, and having a purpose, is knowing that the world does not define who you are. That you, as a child and heir of the King, belong to God. That alone is your identity.

> You are a chosen people. You are royal priests,
> a holy nation, God's very own possession.
> 1 PETER 2:9 NLT

Don't underestimate your role in the grand master plan of life.

"For I know the plans I have for you," declares the LORD, "plans to prosper you and not to harm you, plans to give you hope and a future."
JEREMIAH 29:11 NIV

Don't let your feelings trick you into believing you are alone. You are not.

> The LORD is close to all who call on him,
> yes, to all who call on him in truth.
> PSALM 145:18 NLT

The coolest, most important part of an outfit isn't something you find in a store, salon, or magazine.
It's who you are.

Let your adorning be the hidden person of the heart with the imperishable beauty of a gentle and quiet spirit, which in God's sight is very precious.
1 PETER 3:4 ESV

You are not invisible. You are amazing. God made you and that means you're special.

> We are God's masterpiece. He has created us anew in Christ Jesus, so we can do the good things he planned for us long ago.
> EPHESIANS 2:10 NLT

You might be young, but you're not too young to change the world!

Don't let anyone think less of you because you are young. Be an example to all believers in what you say, in the way you live, in your love, your faith, and your purity.

1 Timothy 4:12 NLT

Sometimes it's hard to see where we fit in or belong. Always be positive and give plenty of compliments—you'll be surprised how many people start telling you how special you are.

> God has placed the parts in the body, every one of them, just as he wanted them to be.... You are the body of Christ, and each one of you is a part of it.
>
> 1 CORINTHIANS 12:18, 27 NIV

Everyone feels lonely now and then. When you do start feeling depressed, whatever you do, talk to someone about it.

Don't be afraid, for I am with you.
Don't be discouraged, for I am your God.
I will strengthen you and help you.
I will hold you up with my victorious right hand.
    Isaiah 41:10 nlt

Sometimes, being awkward and unsure is a good thing; it gives time for the "real" us to emerge and grow and strengthen.

Consider it a sheer gift, friends, when tests and challenges come at you from all sides. You know that under pressure, your faith-life is forced into the open and shows its true colors. So don't try to get out of anything prematurely. Let it do its work so you become mature and well-developed, not deficient in any way.

JAMES 1:2-4 THE MESSAGE

It may sting a little, or you might get in trouble, but it's always better to be honest.

What this adds up to, then, is this: no more lies, no more pretense. Tell your neighbor the truth. In Christ's body we're all connected to each other, after all. When you lie to others, you end up lying to yourself.
        Ephesians 4:25 the message

Some things are unfixable. Those are the things you have to rely on God for. He can give you strength when you're not sure you can get up off the floor.

Come to me, all you who are weary and burdened, and I will give you rest. ...for I am gentle and humble in heart, and you will find rest for your souls.
MATTHEW 11:28-29 NIV

Try to focus on someone other than yourself for a day. Serving others is a great way to take the focus off yourself.

As each has received a gift, use it to serve one another, as good stewards of God's varied grace.
1 Peter 4:10 ESV

The one true friend that you will always be able to count on is Jesus. He'll always be there for you and will never let you down.

> There are "friends" who destroy each other,
> but a real friend sticks closer than a brother.
> PROVERBS 18:24 NLT

You can accomplish anything with God on your side! So get out there and try.

> With people it is impossible, but not with God; for all things are possible with God.
> MARK 10:27 NASB

By studying the Bible, you can see how it speaks to you and applies to what you're going through.

> Your word is a lamp to guide my feet
> and a light for my path.
> PSALM 119:105 NLT

The mere fact that we are grateful for things and giving God credit for them is a form of worship.

Praise the LORD!
Oh give thanks to the LORD for He is good;
For His lovingkindness is everlasting.
PSALM 106:1 NASB

Stay the course; hang in there. God is not playing a game with us, tempting and trying to see where we'll trip up. He is in our corner, rooting for us every second of every day.

> God is faithful; he will not let you be tempted beyond what you can bear.
> 1 Corinthians 10:13 NIV

Knowing someone's heart is at the center of understanding them.

O LORD, you have examined my heart
and know everything about me.
You know when I sit down or stand up.
You know my thoughts even when I'm far away.
　　　　PSALM 139:1-2 NLT

God made us to be active people. He doesn't want us to just sit around and be lazy.

We want each of you to show this same diligence to the very end, so that what you hope for may be fully realized. We do not want you to become lazy, but to imitate those who through faith and patience inherit what has been promised.
   HEBREWS 6:11-12 NIV

True success is measured by how honoring we are to God and by making a difference in the lives of others.

We have no doubts about what we're doing or why, but it's hard going and we need your prayers. All we care about is living well before God.

HEBREWS 13:18 THE MESSAGE

The Bible changes lives.
People are literally changed by
spending time reading the Bible.

All Scripture is inspired by God and is useful to teach us what is true and to make us realize what is wrong in our lives. It corrects us when we are wrong and teaches us to do what is right. God uses it to prepare and equip his people to do every good work.
2 Timothy 3:16-17 NLT

Knowing how much God loves me makes me think I should try to love the way He does.

Love each other. Just as I have loved you, you should love each other.
John 13:34 NLT

The next time life throws you a tragic curve ball, look at it as another step deeper into an intimate understanding of yourself, your family, and your God.

> Anyone who meets a testing challenge head-on and manages to stick it out is mighty fortunate. For such persons loyally in love with God, the reward is life and more life.
>
> JAMES 1:12 THE MESSAGE

God uses lots of small packages to accomplish what He wants.

God's various expressions of power are in action everywhere; but God himself is behind it all. Each person is given something to do that shows who God is: Everyone gets in on it, everyone benefits.

1 Corinthians 12:6-7 the message

If Jesus knew that it was important to pray to God, then we know that it is important for us.

> Whatever things you ask when you pray, believe that you receive them, and you will have them.
>
> MARK 11:24 NKJV

The one good way to avoid whining is to wake up every day and thank God for all the wonderful blessings He has given you and your family. Gratefulness is always the cure for that terrible whining virus.

> Give thanks to the LORD,
> call upon his name....
> Sing praises to the LORD, for he has done gloriously;
> let this be made known in all the earth.
> — Isaiah 12:4–5 ESV

It's not just about following the rules—it's about monitoring your intake. Garbage in = garbage out. Your parents have rules about your phones, video games, and computers to protect you.

> Don't copy the behavior and customs of this world, but let God transform you into a new person by changing the way you think. Then you will learn to know God's will for you, which is good and pleasing and perfect.
> ROMANS 12:2 NLT

The best test for a worthy role model is if their lives reflect the things God says to do and not to do. The Bible is the best measuring stick for your role model.

Blessed is the one...
whose delight is in the law of the LORD,
and who meditates on his law day and night.
That person is like a tree planted by streams of water,
which yields fruit in season
and whose leaf does not wither—
whatever they do prospers.
    PSALM 1:1–3 NIV

God won't leave us to get through it all by ourselves. No matter what we feel or can sense in our desperate moments... God has not abandoned us.

Do not be afraid or discouraged, for the LORD will personally go ahead of you. He will be with you; he will neither fail you nor abandon you.
DEUTERONOMY 31:8 NLT

The wind was created to prove wrong our doubts about God. It is a perfect representation of believing in what we can't see. Although we can't tangibly see the wind, we can feel it unmistakably. Although we cannot physically grasp onto it, we can see its effects when it touches something.

To all who did receive him, who believed in his name, he gave the right to become children of God.
JOHN 1:12 ESV

Respect people the way
you want to be respected.

Here is a simple, rule-of-thumb guide for behavior: Ask yourself what you want people to do for you, then grab the initiative and do it for *them*.

MATTHEW 7:12 THE MESSAGE

Jesus laid down His life for His friends, and He encouraged us to do the same.

This is my command: Love one another the way I loved you. This is the very best way to love. Put your life on the line for your friends.
JOHN 15:12-13 THE MESSAGE

Ask for a clean heart. A new heart. Lay down the old and painful parts, and ask Jesus to heal the wounds once and for all.

Create in me a clean heart, O God,
and renew a right spirit within me.
Cast me not away from your presence,
and take not your Holy Spirit from me.
Restore to me the joy of your salvation,
and uphold me with a willing spirit.
     PSALM 51:10-13 ESV

Great *fullness* is an understanding that all we have and do and are together is beautiful and unique and extra-ordinarily amazing.

How good and pleasant it is
when God's people live together in unity!
PSALM 133:1 NIV

God is always there for you. He can give you strength and support when you need it.

The LORD is my strength and shield.
I trust him with all my heart.
He helps me, and my heart is filled with joy.
I burst out in songs of thanksgiving.
     PSALM 28:7 NLT

Stay strong and work on bringing glory to God. He will do the rest with the talent He's given you.

Not to us, LORD, not to us
but to your name be the glory,
because of your love and faithfulness.
PSALM 115:1 NIV

There *is* something to live for, and we need to make the time we've been given count!

So be careful how you live. Don't live like fools, but like those who are wise. Make the most of every opportunity in these evil days.

Ephesians 5:15-16 nlt

The Lord wants us to know how much He values us individually. He created each person exactly the way He wanted. No mistakes.

My frame was not hidden from you
when I was made in the secret place,
when I was woven together in the depths of the earth.
Your eyes saw my unformed body;
all the days ordained for me were written in your book
before one of them came to be.
        Psalm 139:15-16 niv

Good looks are fleeting. Make-up washes off in the rain. And people's opinions change faster than the wind. God is the same yesterday, today, and tomorrow. He always loves you.

Jesus Christ is the same yesterday, today, and forever. Do not be carried about with various and strange doctrines. For it is good that the heart be established by grace.
Hebrews 13:8-9 NKJV

The world doesn't define who you are; God does.

My heart is confident in you, O God;
my heart is confident.
No wonder I can sing your praises!
PSALM 57:7 NLT

It's really up to you. You have the choice to spend real time with God, and real time with your friends. It will be more than worth every second!

A single day in your courts
is better than a thousand anywhere else!
I would rather be a gatekeeper in the house of my God
than live the good life in the homes of the wicked.
   PSALM 84:10 NLT

We are way too busy not to make the time for God.

I would have despaired unless I had believed
that I would see the goodness of the LORD
In the land of the living.
Wait for the LORD;
Be strong and let your heart take courage;
Yes, wait for the LORD.
　　　　Psalm 27:13-14 nasb

Ask Jesus to come and speak to the pain and the pressure that builds and builds and never seems to fade inside.

> "LORD, help!" they cried in their trouble,
> and he saved them from their distress.
> He sent out his word and healed them,
> snatching them from the door of death.
> PSALM 107:19-20 NLT

You can always talk to God. He desires to have a conversation with you.

Those the Father has given me will come to me, and I will never reject them.
JOHN 6:37 NLT

> God has made Himself completely available for the life moments when we can't make sense of anything or anyone but Him.

God is our refuge and strength,
an ever-present help in trouble.
Therefore we will not fear, though the earth give way
and the mountains fall into the heart of the sea.
        PSALM 46:1-2 NIV

Jesus promised us true life when He came the first time… He offers it to any and all who will risk to trust and begin again. His promise today is to exceed our expectations!

Christ will live in you as you open the door and invite him in. And I ask him that with both feet planted firmly on love, you'll be able to take in with all the followers of Jesus the extravagant dimensions of Christ's love.

Ephesians 3:17-18 THE MESSAGE

Happiness comes from within... never from without. Don't buy into the ageless lie, "If only... then I would be happy."

Take delight in the LORD,
and he will give you the desires of your heart.
Commit your way to the LORD;
trust in him and he will do this.
               PSALM 37:4-5 NIV

> God is our anchor, our hope, and our certainty in an insane world.

We who have fled to him for refuge can have great confidence as we hold to the hope that lies before us. This hope is a strong and trustworthy anchor for our souls.

HEBREWS 6:18-19 NLT

The most effective way to communicate is in what our actions say... not our words.

> Dear children, let's not merely say that we love each other; let us show the truth by our actions.
>
> 1 John 3:18 NLT

Have confidence in yourself no matter what people say to you. Always look to God because He's the only one that matters in the end.

If you brag, brag of this and this only:
That you understand and know me.
I'm GOD, and I act in loyal love.
I do what's right and set things right and fair,
and delight in those who do the same things.
   JEREMIAH 9:24 THE MESSAGE

When you understand that God has so much of a plan for you, it gives your life so much more meaning.

> A good woman is hard to find,
> and worth far more than diamonds.
> PROVERBS 31:10 THE MESSAGE